-A1

1

Double Drivel

By

Ed Chandler

For ALL the Poets

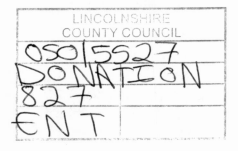

Contents

Introduction

I could argue that if this is the '**In**troduction' then there must be an **Out** 'ro-duct-ion'?

As the opposite of 'In' is 'Out' surely that would make some sense, but no sense at all.

And so we're back again, it's Drivel Twice or the more appropriate title of "Double Drivel", because my intention was that, what I've put together was just as much Drivel as I did last time only this time I've added just a few extra things and covered some old ground as well as finding some new ground to play on or with?

Are you still with me?

Good as I never actually thought I'd write a second book, or even a follow on to "Drivel". I guess this was a 'second thought' in that I'd some sort of an idea that I could write another book with a load of 'Drivel' in it, but it would stand alone from the first book, but also have some odd little references and points going back to the first, thus making it "Double Drivel". So read on and I'll tell you all about my...

Missed Bits

The main reason for calling this chapter 'Missed Bits' wasn't only to a deliberately tell you about a fortuitous error in the first book 'Drivel' but also some of the other things I often foolishly do when typing all these words, so do bare or 'bear' with me...

Because, 'Missed Bits' is what they were, just that, not only did I miss a word out in the last book, it's on Page Thirty-five, as I'm about to tell you. The other thing was this gave me an opportunity to throw together the last few oddments and random lines I'd collected on my writing adventures, also I might have actually discovered just exactly how many Tigers there are in England. Then again I might not and as we've some more questions to come and some fun with déjà vu and all that, I have to ponder, is this 'Double Drivel' going to be twice as much fun as the first one was, or will it be twice as bad?

My very lovely mum first pointed out that in the previous book to this, 'Drivel' that on Page Thirty-five I miss out the word "gun" from the James Bond film title "The Man with the Golden Gun", now this was in some small part a deliberate, but also it was an accidental error. You see, I'm the only one who edits all this rubbish, as I don't have the luxury of an editor yet, not while I write this, so if I go wrong, if I spell something incorrectly, then I rely on the computer to underline it in red, green if it's grammar and blue means I've typed the wrong word, but this doesn't always happen.

Take my "quiet" and "quite". 'Quite' that is to refer to something 'fairly' or 'pretty' and 'moderately' according to the computers Thesaurus, whereas "quiet" is more 'calm' and 'soft', so when I mean to say it was all "quiet" as in there was no sound or something, but I accidently type "quite", which is wrong, then I have to laugh and say, well we all make mistakes, it's all part of being human.

Also for some reason I thought the word 'luxury' was spelt "luctury", no idea how I got that?

Maybe it was because how I was saying it and then thinking on how I would spell it, so I made the word sound in my head and said 'luxury' out loud, but it sounds more to me something like:- "Looked- Jury".

Think on that for a moment and say 'luxury' back to yourself then say 'looked-jury' together really fast...

It was then I realise, it's nothing at all, a bit like the word 'yourself' as it's one word and not two. So you see then there are some disadvantages to just producing a book all by yourself and not having someone look over it before it goes to full copy and sits on a shelf for someone to come and buy or borrow and then read and only to discover that you miss out something, or you use 'quite' and not 'quiet' and then I thought well you could hardly call that an error, just more a simple mistake. After all to miss it out might be intentional, but not to miss it out without a doubt is just a plain mistake.

It did it again then, as 'without' is also one word, I just found out, how silly of me, as I should know these things, right?

I did do English at school, which was some time ago now, as I'm thirty-two now, so do please forgive the odd little mistake, sometimes I don't realise I make or made them and others I do, but then I think, hang on a moment, I could have some fun with that...

As why is 'without' and 'yourself' all one word, but the word 'some-time' is two words?

Dam it, that's a question, I'm supposed to leave those until later...

You see there's another thing about missing bits or not putting bits in, I was at the Tennyson Research Centre a few days ago in April of the year two-thousand and fifteen. I was looking at some of the books that Alfred Lord Tennyson wrote and there are notes to his own poems after they were published and bits that were just simply cut out.

If I write something and then think that's no good, I might cut and paste it into a blank word document and save it for another day, or I might simply delete it and then it's gone. For that is the beauty of the

9

printed word, typing it all out digitally or electronically, you can chop and change it as you go, edit and re-edit without the dear reader having ever known.

It's like the gaze of a man's eyes, for he sees the beauty around him and doesn't know where to look on summer's day as breasts and bums are displayed in neat little costumes. Any and almost every man looks.

After all we men don't have bosoms to admire, so we must indulge ourselves by looking at the busts of those ladies we pass and to whom some might notice and others won't. Such is the great endeavour and why men hardly ever understand women, if not at all and why women can sometimes struggle to understand us men.

The opposite sex...

I bought a girlfriend of mine some naughty knickers once, you know lingerie and all that, I thought it was a very nice gesture, turns out buying ones that had written on it "In case of emergency, pull down" wasn't that good an idea, although there was a moment of humour, however it was soon replaced with a scornful look...

Women are missed out all the time, as for a woman to have done the crime could have been seen to be wrong not that long ago, look back at history to see the mystery of women unfold.

Ladies you're all very lovely and I thank you for skimpy outfits, pert behinds, full bosoms and beautiful eyes, a vast and far superior intelligence, a glowing look, a great way with words and men. Without the two sexes, life on Earth would be dull especially if there were no 'sex' at all.

There's a girl with flowers in her hair...

My lady is in a winter's scene on a summer's day.

Can we change direction with Missed Bits, for I was on about women, but could I now throw in something completely different?

I really should stop putting in these questions, when all questions should come at the end, or at least within the chapter of "Second Questions".

Only I didn't want to miss anything out this time, so I thought I'd best get it in now while I was on this chapter, before we so quickly move onto the next one...

I was communicating my thoughts on to the keyboard of letters before me, making them into words and watching them appear onto the screen before me, when I made a slight error and the green, red or even blue line appeared. I'd wait until I'd reached the end of that paragraph or point in writing before going back over what I'd just written to first see that it at least made some sense to me and that I could read it, for I figure if I can read it then at least you should be able to.

After the paragraph was done and the errors or slight mistakes fixed, I'd look at some old hand written notes or put my brain into gear, if that were even possible, but still it's a nice expression, suggesting the human brain is like that of a car engine and you can select the right gear to get the right response from your own mind.

Only before I go, I must murder words, for they let me down a bit, well I think the spell-check I rely on did, for I wrote what I thought is a good Murder Mystery, it has a good plot and story, get's you guessing who did the crime, but sadly I go from "George" to 'Gorge' as a person and a 'Weeding' not a 'Wedding' takes place...

We preamble then as I introduce the next instalment and we inspire with words and I look forward, not foreword with a book, but instead a Post-script and 'pre'-script at the same time. It's the end of the chapter, but not the end of the book, so please do read on and continue into my...

Preamble

You know what I'm going to suggest right?

'Pre' and not 'Post'...

Forgive the change in font, as just to mix things up, I thought why not. In fact each chapter will begin in a different 'type' or font to that of the previous chapter.

Just a small thought, but why is 'in fact' two words and not all 'one'?

I see a man I don't know. The police will come if I kill him now. Is it all inconsequential? Is death really that bad?

Forget the ellipses and go on to the square route of things. Often when you are looking for a word, just as I looked for 'Ellipses' in a dictionary, on the other page before it was the word 'ejaculate' which of course has it's main sexual meaning, but also has a secondary meaning of "To utter 'something'".

Therefore I can 'ejaculate' my words. I shall whisper them to you and place the words upon this page, rather than in any other book of mine. I shall move the 'plant' machinery that removes weeds and helps to cultivate flowers, fruit like tomatoes and vegetables like potatoes and carrots. At no extra cost I can afford the luxury of a new plant to mechanise my 'plant' machinery and that shall be the bulldozer and digger to a future of bold new words, poetry, both short and long stories that become great novels that shall live on long after I'm gone.

I read this thing once, written in 1826, it described 'Kissing' as "A novel method first introduced on Friday morning last, by an Ape escaped from one of the Plantations at C-I-N-K"

I'm not entirely sure what or if 'C-I-N-K' is a person or a place, but still to suggest that 'kissing' is a novel thing and first thought of by an 'Ape'. Well any writer should be able to make something of that, I hope.

I've no plot, this is not erotic and as my tigers play and I see the sun rise and fall each and every day.

I'm fed up of putting the letter 'I' in the wrong place, often the 'point' of the matter is spelt wrong, I get my 'main' issues all incorrect and the red line appears once more to taunt me.

I should know better English and practice more or at least not type so fast or make a mistake. I could then forget it or not tell you I'd made an error and then over look it as I press 'F7' on my keyboard and the computer begins to tell me of all my little errors. I correct them accordingly and hope there are no more...

I'm off to the book shop to buy a 'Pop Up' book on sexual intercourse, just to see if I get a 'rise' out of it.

I'm playing with murder on my mind, trying to conjure up another idea for another book, while all the time I write this one.

I leave behind the play and pantomime, for often I can create a story, a plot or base of an idea, put the characters together in a setting, but then as I think on what they should say, no words befall me and the characters remain silent. Perhaps that itself would make a good scene in a play as the characters wait for the writer to hand them the script, so that they might talk and speak.

If I get stuck then all I have to do is find some more words.

There are these cheese-maker moments, a point of reference, a solitary flower in bloom, the only candle that lit the room. It's all in here and all out there.

Where you find it and how you use it, is entirely up to you. It's the will to write and the joy of life.

If the first ten pages captures the reader, then after that don't let them go, carry on with good humour, deadly plot, suspense, thrills, power, potions, people and the characters that come to life. It's your piece of work, so you make it how you want.

If I've 'Captured' this reader, then where are they, and had I better not release them before I'm convicted of kidnapping?

Let us return to the amber glow of dawn. In the morning as the sun is upon us, it's now night-time for the night-worker.

For I never remain silent when I talk.

I could've gone anywhere, but I sat here with my eyes closed thinking and then after awhile I began to write.

I'm here, but not here, because I'm supposed to be here.

Only if I'm here and not there, but here and there or here, then I'm here, but not here and nor there or here.

As I continued into each chapter, I decided that six pages per each should do, except of course my

Introduction and Epilogue, the rest have six pages each.

Keeping things short and sweet is often a treat.

When you're way down in the dark depths of despair, just think there's bound to be someone a lot worse off than you!

Books can change people's lives, or so they tell me and perhaps some of my books might just do that, for have you read any of the "Run Of The Mill" series in which I try to explore that:-

"Life Is A Two Letter Word."

Mainly for the simple reason that the word 'If' can be found right in the middle of the word life, but then I think I've said that before, so it's...

Déjà Vu

Do you ever get 'déjà vu' when someone tells you something that you already must have heard?

In fact there is a very good film that does the whole déjà vu thing really good, it's called 'Groundhog Day' and it sees the actor and comedian Bill Murray living the same day over and over again, or repeatedly. It's a very good film, but let us not dwell too much on that for now.

Going back again I find the word 'type' is both for 'kind' and 'font', 'brand' or 'print'. Showing that one word can have different meanings, remember it's not the **minute** that counts.

Now you can read that as "minute" as in a 'moment' or "minute" as in 'extremely small'. I checked the dictionary, they're both spelt the same. I get all these crazy ideas and sometimes I've nothing to do with them, but to jot them all down and come back to them later, it's not the case of repeating myself and nor am I lost in translation, baffled by the realisation that this is all just déjà vu to you.

It's like the waterfall, each drop soon reaches me.

Water:

I'm sat listening to the sound of a waterfall,
As water crashes onto rock,
And water gushes into a pool,
It crashes and disturbs the calm,
The water wildly crusades along,
It flows into a stream, meanders as a brook,
From dripping of the rocks,
To moving into the river,
The water flows on and out to sea.

There is vigour in my words, just as water from
the brook and tap. My words are flowing like
water from the river, as rain falls from the sky
to fill up the channel, I fill the page with more
stuff and nonsense, but it's all relative to me,
you, him or her, them and us and to the human
race.

For perhaps we're not alone after all in this
great and vast universe and it's only a matter of
time before another life-form, possibly like us,
will come to visit and say hello.

This book is not without a plot or theme, it's no
dream, it's merely something for one to enjoy.
It's for you to contemplate on and to think and
admire, or to merely use to wipe ones behind
with or to start a fire on a cold windswept moor
perhaps.

There's no use and many a use for this book, so simply read on. Because, whatever you do with this book, if you inflict it upon a family member or a friend as some cruel and twisted gift, buy it for your 'Secret Santa' present or borrow it from the Library, if they still exist.

No matter what, I simply ask that all you do is take something or perhaps nothing at all from this 'Double Drivel', this second tie of emotions, a complex illusion and fusion of lyrics, hidden in a eulogy of time, space, words, letters arranged altogether in sentences and paragraphs that become the page and follow onto a new chapter of great beginnings and endings.

For we are all doomed and destined to die...

Life is not all cuckoo clocks and chocolate, beer, boobs, body, soul and debauchery. Life is what you make it.

This is what I know and I'm using it as best as I can to make something and nothing all in one. That's what I know and I'm abusing it as often as I can, to make it into nothing and something all in one.

If there is a moment of déjà vu and if there is not one, then it shouldn't matter, for life is all a game in one respect, and who knows if you'll be here tomorrow or even the day after that.

Sometimes we live for the moment in the moment, we can plan our respective future and plans can change.

Do you recall the fall of it all, as I lost you in the words and found you on this page, going back to see if I'd told you this before?

Do we not recollect too much and remind ourselves of past indiscretions and focus on a past that's often better off left forgotten, not that we should learn from our mistakes, but sometimes it's just best to simply move on.

I've got a dissonance theory to all this, it's just a case of not repeating one's self and you just have to live life as best as you can, that's all. As if nothing really matters once you're dead and buried or have been cremated.

You might get to leave something or someone behind and then again you might not. If anything I'm inconsistent and so often is life.

We can be lazy, if we take the time, we can achieve many great things, we can write, we can teach, we can pass on what we've learnt so that the next generation might do better.

We shall forever and ever endeavour, we shall no longer wilfully destroy the very planet that gives us so much as we return it with so little.

Perhaps I'm destined to be dust on the wind, left forgotten in some book, a worn out photograph, a Facebook page, a golden moment on screen, in television drama, as the first man to set foot on Jupiter. Only I'm nothing but me and I line up my words into an array of unusual moments that appear like déjà vu, for you think you've read or seen it somewhere before perhaps? There's a notion to a once forgotten and ancient writer, to the influence that even I didn't notice. I recall, I digest, I'm like a moment on 'Groundhog Day' as I wait for the shadow and the forthcoming of spring, I know what's about to happen, for I've been here before and if I choose to change something, do I change myself or do I change those around me?

I was feeling the brunt of my alterations, deciding if I'd covered it all before I moved on, finding the very last few words to make the sixth page, flicking through forgotten and stashed away notebooks, looking at dates scribed in ink, this part is from a mystic exultation, lost in nineteen seventy-three, back to you and not me. I continue to 'Double Drivel' and with promiscuity I write.

As Prince John held the florescent lamp in the year 1185, I was at Baronial Castle. I took a Griffon Vulture and flew off with the tide. The monogamous birds come back in summer, Botticelli sings an Opera and I write a book.

You live your life and we all sing together.

We're on the sixth page and I'm lost, for what else can I say, if nothing but a single word flows, should it be déjà vu?

I've seen the spotted flycatchers on my way home as I went to buy a yellow hammer and as the cage and the gadget are with the travelling man...

None of these perhaps have anything in common and they could be just but a few lines, only they could be the inspiration you've been looking for, or perhaps it's more a case of déjà vu and then again perhaps it's not, for I must continue. I must take up my hand and place my fingers onto the keyboard, press the letters to form words, go back and correct where the green, blue and red line appears and then venture forth once more before I say "Now I might <u>repeat</u> myself, but then I only <u>repeat</u> myself for I might have something good to say, or at least write down before I ask myself some..."

SECOND QUESTIONS

I realised that I must have some more questions, only what would they be? And why on earth do I keep on asking them?

I guess it's all a part of life, for we all have questions, it's just a case of if we have the answers or not. And who can say that the answer we do have is even right? Or perhaps correct? It's a little bit like any rhyme doing any crime for being in a poem that does not tell you the time.

And so I ask myself...

Am I lost? Are you lost?

Should the question be: Are "we" lost?

What are we going to do about **it**?

24

As if 'it' refers to being 'lost' in this case, but perhaps 'it' can presume many an identity?

Think about who is who and what is what if you will, decide where is 'where' and when was that? But most of all let me tell you how I came to now...

As I've no idea where **that** will be? And I don't know the name of the game.

For how shall we know which is which, or what is what?

When the bells ring, do you sing?

What colour is the dark of night?

When the chalk dust settles, then what? The thing is, "What does teacher do at night...?

Will tomorrow ever come?

When more than one tiger you can see,
Then run best ye,
Or else you'll be the tiger's tea...

When you come home and it's raining, do you cry?

Why are we so afraid of the dark?
Who is that person?
Where is the poem?
When is the sun going to shine?
How much do the books weigh?

Has anyone got my fish?
Did I even have a fish?

When is it time?
Is this really a book?
Don't you know you're crazy?

Why does he keep on asking these daft questions?

Did no one ever tell you, you can be anything you want to be!

Do you speak Italian? For I want to translate my poem, I want to sing a vast Opera, but I don't know enough Italian to make it sound good. I think of words that sound Italian, but are most likely not.

'Dolce amore, to Vida est. bon sue-fee-la..."

It means to me that:-

'Your love is great and good, for ever more!"

Only none of its likely to be Italian, but then I can suppose my fiction and make up things as I go along, it's somewhat the "Writers

Prerogative", for to oppose and repose the question, to go into the dark and come out of the light, to venture, to gain, to be or not to do any more, is that the question?

Does anybody know what we are living for?
Can you hear them in the park?
Why is 'it' there?
How many benches are there in the Dawber Garden?

Do all the Prime Ministers of England get to live at 10 Downing Street? If you were Prime Minister, then what?

I was once asked as part of the start to a poem or short story:-

"IF your life was a jar of pickle, what kind of pickle would you be?

I guess you can change the jar of pickle to another object, but to write from the point of view of something that does nothing, isn't difficult, but could be a worthwhile challenge.

Do you want some eggs? I don't want any...

I like the idea of going into any supermarket and asking, 'How many baked beans are there in this tin? For should the staff member know, should anybody know exactly how many baked beans there would be in a four hundred gram can? Perhaps someone will have to count them.

If you don't ask daft questions every now and then, or pose the thought of even plausible questions, then without any questions, we would no longer have anything to ask...

Can you imagine that, living in a world where you knew everything, I mean there are search engines on the internet that will aim to tell you as much as they can when you type something into the search engine and then look for it, so try your name or mine, or his or hers. Try a random question like asking 'How many Monkeys are there at London Zoo?' or perhaps we might return to the number of Tigers in England and why miss out Wales, Scotland and then both Northern Ireland and Ireland, should there be any Tigers on the Isle of Man or White?

How did a Tiger find itself in tree?

Do I make sense, but no sense at all? For this 'Double Drivel', this ramble of words, this collection of letters, this page, this book, it's all for you to enjoy and digest, take in and take apart, to laugh at, to ridicule, to wipe your tears away and not for your behind, <u>but</u> for the rubbish pile, the funeral pyre, a great fire to keep you warm while sheltering from the storm. It is then I've no more questions at this point and so I move back to my...

Drivel

Drivel which is to say more of nonsense and good old foolishness and lots of rubbish all piled into what is more poppycock than anything else. My idiocy which is neither the blame and nor the cause of this claptrap that's to follow, for I have my sense and yet I've no sense at all. For all my sense was gone, taken in the night by some thief, in fact **Don Drivel** was the mob man who did all the taking in those days, I was just the hit man, fed up of all the dirty work, having to deal with the tosh and turmoil of death and danger, dealing with drugs and laundering money.

One morning back in July, it was the fifteenth I recall for St Swithen's bells rang out and the rain was not to be seen, for should it have rained on St Swithen's day, then the fable says it shall rain for Forty days and nights more.

I'm just a lonely henchman, the man of deeds, I fulfil Don Drivel's needs, I kill those who oppose him and dine at his request. I debauched women and sought pleasure in the dark of night. Only I'm no longer content with the evil and crimes of Don Drivel, I'm fed up. I seek my revenge. I'll get him and then I'll set myself free. Time passes and a note arrives, it was from the Don, he beckoned me that summer's day. He left a note in Italian, translated it read:-

"Next time don't eat alone.'

He referred to the fact that I'd gone to a local establishment for a good meal, when I should've gone to his home. Only I didn't feel like going to his home, I felt like killing him.

I knew there were others who wanted to get rid of Don Drivel and so if I 'bumped' him off then how could the blame fall with me? I had it all planned, I could make out I was at a football match, in the Don's private box, while he'd be at home all alone, I could sneak away from the game and then make a call to him while on my way. I knew his phones had been bugged by the police and other Law Enforcement Agencies, so by having the background noise of the football match in the milieu, while I made my call, I'd have an alibi.

Only I didn't figure on some clever Detective, who put a few small things together. You see I used a Security Company Van as cover to leave the match and it was spotted near the Don's house, also in the private box is a clock that strikes upon the half hour, quarter-to or quarter past of the hour, I called at just before half past two in the afternoon, but the sound of the clock was not heard on the tape. Simple, my excuse was that the call was short and therefore, you wouldn't here the clock chime and also the clock was a little slow, so my call was ended before it chimed at two-thirty. I'd therefore gotten away with 'Murder'.

I pause for gin and juice.

Have you seen the film "Willy Wonka And The Chocolate Factory", the one where

Gene Wilder plays Willy Wonka, it was on television the other day, well it was when I wrote this...

Anyway, in the film when Charlie finds the last golden ticket, what gets me is how does 'Slugworth' know he's just found it, as a few moments after finding the ticket, there he is, good old 'Mr Slugworth' asking Charlie to get an everlasting gobstopper. If you've got the nineteen seventy-one film of "Willy Wonka And The Chocolate Factory" then watch it and try to work out just how it's done, just for fun...

There's a great deal of difference between who 'knows' and how my 'nose' got into all this, but then if 'knows' and 'nose' sound alike I wonder if we can have some fun with that?

For in the middle of it all there I was, lost in loneliness. I'm confused by everything, looking for something or someone.

I was taken away by it all after hiding in the backdrop, amongst the many books, media and a passing Security Guard. The Lincolnshire Life of Wesley Historical Society and a railway that leads to nowhere, but arrives everywhere, as if the poems end...

It's this book of poems, "Penguin's Poems For Life", as if Penguins can read! They do however taste good covered in chocolate...

The Conning Tower, were I was once conned...

Never use two words when one will do...

The Pylons are walking across the land...

Science has killed Romance. Police are looking for witness's to help them identify anyone suspected of anything. There's an invasion of fear, so be prepared and ready for action!

It's as if Human has become a swear word.

The three legged chicken is in the fashionable place to live. The strategy of the soliloquy in the complex idiom is that all problems spurn from one seed into the tree of all problems.

If you want to become a predator then start by knowing your prey. If you've motive, then use it perhaps on your intended victim, it'd be a good start in any 'Murder' based book.

Life and the universe unfold in a desperate nightmare of everlasting love.

Every time I stab the butter with a knife, it makes a sound.

There's no gold or communication,
It's the code of love, but the look of love,
Will get you every time...

So throw me a lifeline and wipe off,
The foundation of lies, this much is true.
Heaven is a secret, it's also a place on Earth.

There were Cows in the Cafe and I had Ice Cream on a rainy day. I was lost in spring as daffodils bloom and birds sing.

Clouds hung inside the roof, there was 'spray' on the road, the puddles linger, as I sit on a worn out leather chair and an umbrella lays at my feet. There's livestock on the blinds, as farm animals block out the window and the view. A silver birch, the little red tractor, a bird box and a girl with flowers in her hair, only don't stare, for I compare it all to a summer's day, a rose, as I prose into poetry. In fact I move towards the number...

Seven

You might begin to wonder why I'm forever changing font, but then in some books to just continue in the same font would be advantageous, but then repetitive. Especially when it comes to poetry, for if each poem had its own font or type, then each poem would stand out by itself. Yes one could easily repeat the font later on with a different poem, but perhaps not on the same page and so I decided to start each chapter with a different font and then end with my Epilogue all in a font of its own...

This chapter is called 'Seven' because this chapter is the seventh in this book and also because at the time I couldn't conceive a better title for the chapter. It occurred to me that although today was my birthday both backwards and forwards for today is fifteen seven fifteen, [15/07/15]. It was then perhaps I could say I had a better idea for the title of this chapter, but decided to remain with calling it 'Seven'. It also had seven pages to it...

Just as this book is 'Double Drivel' and not called "Twice As Much Drivel" or "Drivel Two" or even "Secondary Drivel".

I did call the second 'Run Of The Mill' book I wrote "Secondary Run Of the Mill" as opposed to an original idea of calling it "Not Another Run Of The Mill", this was because I'd already decided to write a trilogy of books and I can promise you now that there won't be a 'Third Lot Of Drivel' hitting the shelves any time soon.

I'd have to think of a better title for a third book based around the 'Drivel' in my head, any suggestions? Or should I stop writing all this stuff and nonsense and get back to something good, like a Murder Mystery or my book about a Detective in the Netherlands just before and then during as well as after the Second World War.

Something different...

The owl wore a scarf, the badger a jacket...

The fox wore a pair of shoes, the cow wore glasses. The duck wore a hat and the lamb wore a woolly jumper. The Pig wore his trotters and the dog wore a tie.

When writing, you'll often find a moment to reflect and look at your surroundings, it's at these times when almost any words can come to mind, if only you write down what you see...

Trees:

Not quite the view I was looking for,
The City amongst the trees
The green has grown around
Red brick buildings, a university complex,
A single grey shed with a black door.
I stand alone and look towards the new
Siemens works, bathed in sunlight,
But ugly in appearance...
To my left is the far hill of Bracebridge Heath
In front is a wide valley,
And to my right there are just trees.

So get those words rumbling around in your head down onto paper...

Keep your chin up and always smile, for even if you only self-publish, at least you'll have your book and that's better than not having any book at all, isn't it?

For to write is to write and to wrong, too wrong and any more nonsense or ideal philosophy, to me it's simple. If you want to write and have a book, then write it, you can access editors and proofreaders, you can self-publish for free and you can hold your head above all others who struggle to get there book out there, for here is yours and here now is my...

Epilogue

Well I'd best start by saying thank you to my mum. Thank you Karen Chandler, my lovely mum and thank you to you the dear reader once more.

Thank you for putting up with all the changes in font, but then it's not 'Drivel' it's double and so on and to the confusion, but to subtract from the boredom I mixed it all up. I started with the first letter of the alphabet and chose "Arial" and then had "Book Antiqua" followed by "Candara", now there was no type beginning with the letter "D" so I went onto "Estrangelo Edssa" then "Franklin Gothic Book" and then "Georgia" now from here to "Latha" it got tricky as there was no H and as for I, J or K well I didn't like them. Back to the alphabet and "Mangal" sadly there was no letter N or O, so it's "Palatino Linotype" and lastly "Raavi", now I had to keep the same size text throughout and decided that the letter size 13 was better than 12 or 14, for 14 was too big and 12 a little too small with some of the fonts used. I know it's bad of me to do this, but thank you for sticking with it and after all it's different and it's "Double Drivel".

Thank you then to all the readers of good old books and not on tablets or by audio, but by good old book, I say thank you to you. It doesn't matter how you are reading this book or if you have listened to it, I still say thank you. Thank you to those at Boultham Library again, as if it weren't for the Chocolate Sunday, Strawberry Monday, Pancake Tuesday, Ash Wednesday, Turkey Thursday, Fish Friday and Sweet Saturday, whatever my week, I'd always find time to go to the Library. Thank you.

Thank you to me and not to him.

Thank you to my Epilogue, as at first I couldn't get the Computers Thesaurus to find it, so I had to use the good old fashioned way and look it up in a paperback book, for I'm a paperback writer...

Sadly I couldn't find my 'Epilogue' in any of the four 'Thesauruses' I had!

I did however find this word: - Ephemeral, which goes on with the words: Brief, transient, evanescent, fleeting, passing, momentary, occasional, short-lived and temporary.

So now I conclude with all my epigrammatic mistakes and errors put to one side, I end and say thanks once more as I draw to an epoch and my age carries forward and not 'foreword'.

Instead I simply mark time, like I mark paper with pen or type to page. With font on computer screen, for my words are here (Not hear) and no longer in my head. Thank you and farewell.

Take care and all the best.

(Place for Autograph #)

\#

\# *Ed Chandler.*

\#

\# *:)*

Ed Chandler

Printed in Great Britain
by Amazon